Belongs to page

_____

_____

_____

Color Test Page

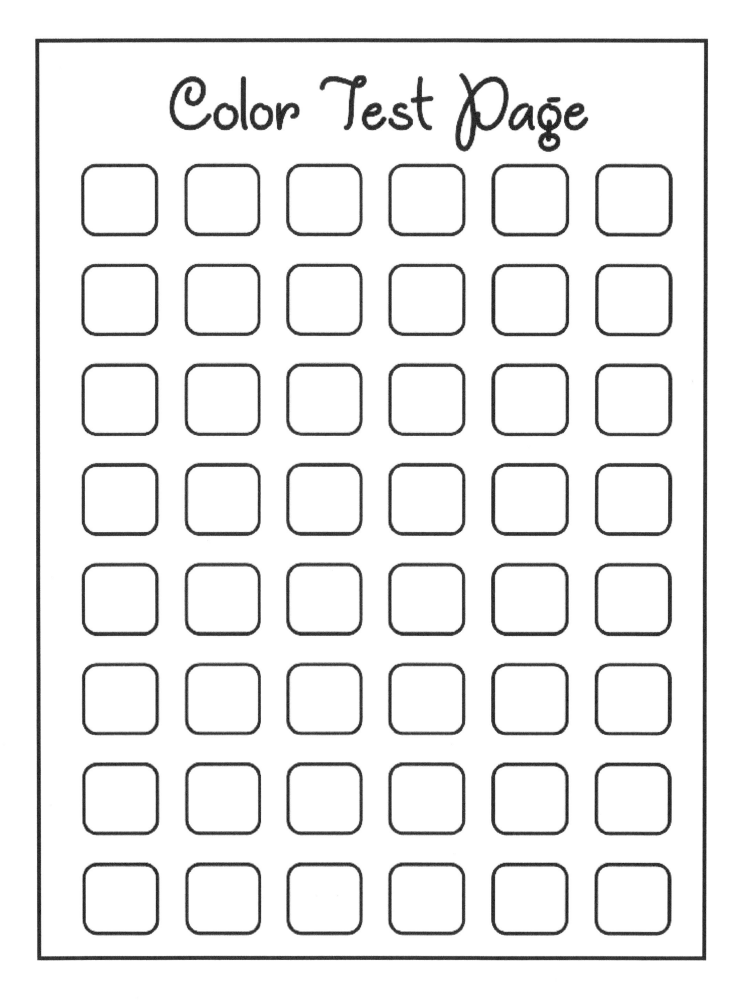

"When we strive to become better than we are, everything around us becomes better too." — Paulo Coelho

"Opportunity is missed by most people because it is dressed in overalls and looks like work." — Thomas Edison

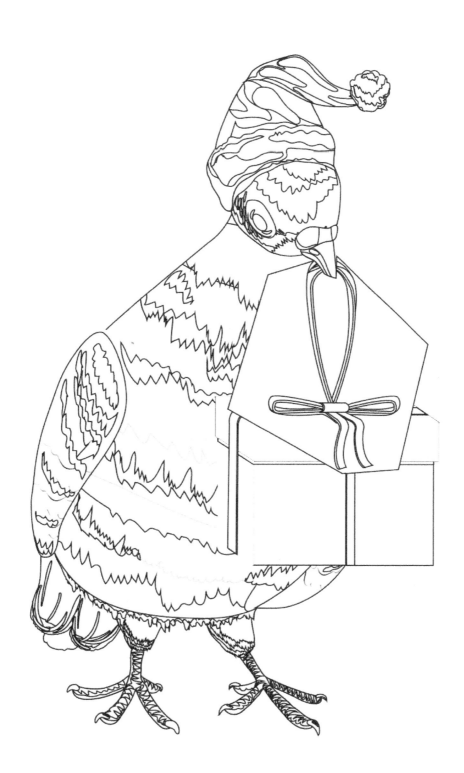

Women challenge the status quo because we are never it." — Cindy Gallop

"Setting goals is the first step in turning the invisible into the visible." — Tony Robbins

We don't just sit around and wait for other people. We just make, and we do."
— Arlan Hamilton

"Think like a queen. A queen is not afraid to fail. Failure is another stepping stone to greatness." — Oprah Winfrey

"Whenever you see a successful woman, look out for three men who are going out of their way to try to block her."
– Yulia Tymoshenko

"The thing women have yet to learn is nobody gives you power. You just take it. " – Roseanne Barr

"To know how much there is to know is the beginning of learning to live." — Dorothy West

"No woman wants to be in submission to a man who isn't in submission to God!"
— T D Jakes

"A witty woman is a treasure; a witty beauty is a power." — George Meredith

"When a woman becomes her own best friend life is easier." – Diane Von Fursten-berg

"If you want something said, ask a man; if you want something done, ask a woman." – Margaret Thatcher

"Women must learn to play the game as men do." – Eleanor Roosevelt

"He who conquers himself is the mightiest warrior." — Confucius

"Try not to become a man of success, but rather become a man of value." – Albert Einstein

"One man with courage makes a majority." – Andrew Jackson

"One secret of success in life is for a man to be ready for his opportunity when it comes." – Benjamin Disraeli

"To know how much there is to know is the be-ginning of learning to live." —Dorothy West

"Experience is a hard teacher because she gives the test Þrst, the lesson afterwards." — Vernon Sanders Law

"If you are working on something that you really care about, you don't have to be pushed. The vision pulls you." — Steve Jobs

"Don't let yesterday take up too much of today." — Will Rogers

"Success is getting what you want, happiness is wanting what you get." - W. P. Kinsella

"I never dreamed about success. I worked for it." —Estée Lauder

"Develop success from failures. Discouragement and failure are two of the surest stepping stones to success." —Dale Carnegie

"Success usually comes to those who are too busy looking for it." — Henry David Thoreau

"Don't let yesterday take up too much of today." — Will Rogers

"Christmas isn't a season. It's a feeling."
—Edna Ferber

"May you never be too grown up to search the skies on Christmas Eve."

"I stopped believing in Santa Claus when I was six. Mother took me to see him in a department store and he asked for my autograph." – Shirley Temple

"Christmas is a piece of one's home that one carries in one's heart." – Freya Stark

"City sidewalks, busy sidewalks, dressed in holiday style. In the air, there's a feeling of Christmas." – Ray Evans, "Silver Bells"

"I will honour Christmas in my heart, and try to keep it all the year." – Charles Dickens, A Christmas Carol

"Christmas is not a time nor a season, but a state of mind. To cherish peace and goodwill, to be plenteous in mercy, is to have the real spirit of Christmas." – Calvin Coolidge

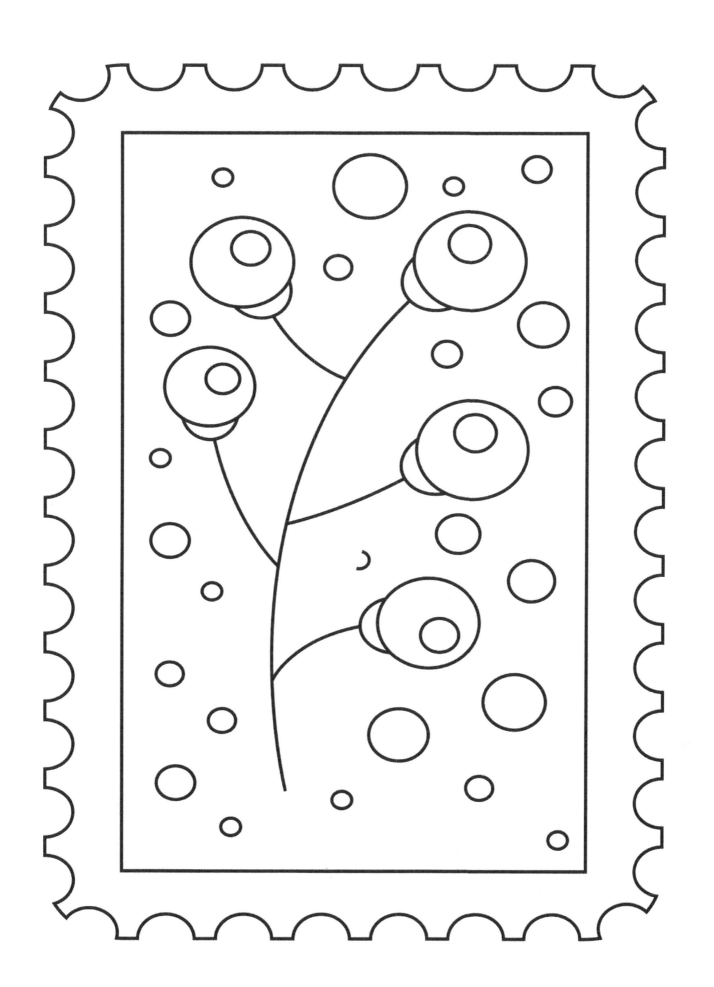

"Some Christmas tree ornaments do a lot more than glitter and glow, they represent a gift of love given a long time ago." – Tom Baker

"The smells of Christmas are the smells of childhood." – Richard Paul Evans

"The thing about Christmas is that it almost doesn't matter what mood you're in, or what kind of year you've had–it's a fresh start." – Kelly Clarkson

"The smells of Christmas are the smells of childhood." – Richard Paul Evans

"The thing about Christmas is that it almost doesn't matter what mood you're in, or what kind of year you've had–it's a fresh start." – Kelly Clarkson

"I love the excitement, the childlike spirit of innocence, and just about everything that goes along with Christmas." – Hillary Scott

"The way you spend Christmas is far more important than how much." – Henry David Thoreau

"Christmas, to me, is as many people as possible happy." – Tupac Shakur

"Even as an adult, I still find it hard to sleep on Christmas eve." – Carrie Latet

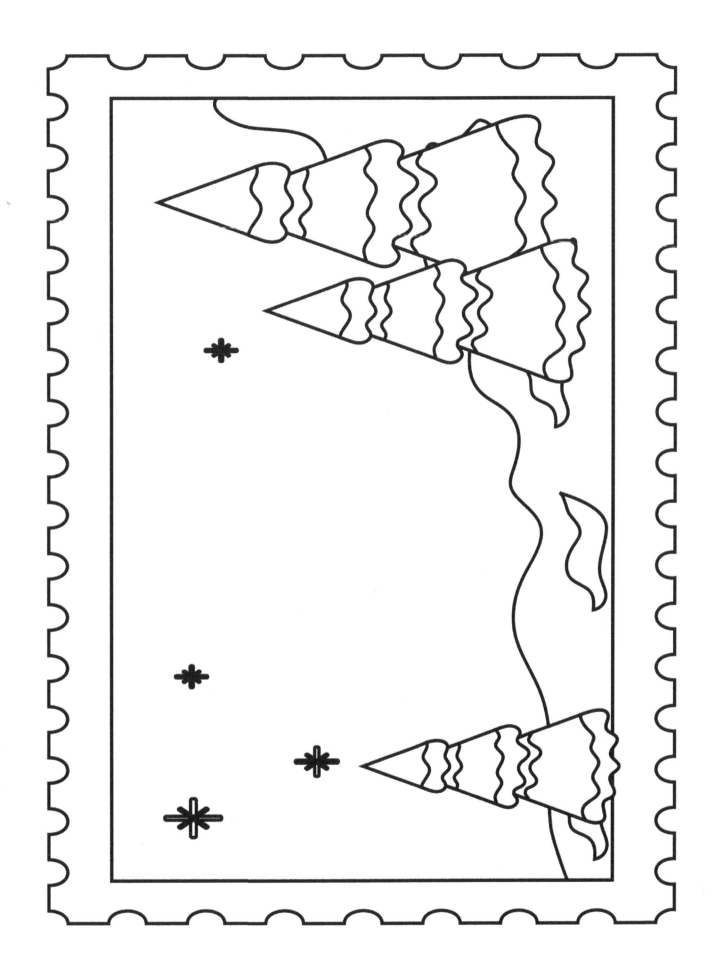

"Christmas is doing a little something extra for someone." – Charles M. Schulz

"Christmas is doing a little something extra for someone." – Charles M. Schulz

"Peace on earth will come to stay, when we live Christmas every day." – Helen Steiner Rice

"Christmas is a day of meaning and traditions, a special day spent in the warm circle of family and friends." – Margaret Thatcher

"The joy of brightening other lives becomes for us the magic of the holidays."
– W. C. Jones

"Christmas magic is silent. You don't hear it–you feel it. You know it. You believe it." – Kevin Alan Milne

Made in United States
Orlando, FL
11 December 2024

55333285R00057